Eight Journals
A Sampler

HARAV AVRAHAM YITZCHAK
HACOHEN KOOK

Translated by Yaacov David Shulman

ISBN: 9798612565420

RAV KOOK'S CREDO

If you desire, human being, look at the light of God's Presence in everything.

Look at the Eden of spiritual life, at how it blazes into each corner and crevice of life, spiritual and of this world, right before your eyes of flesh and your eyes of soul.

Gaze at the wonders of creation, at their divine life--not like some dim phenomenon that is placed before your eyes from afar.

But know the reality in which you live.

Know yourself and your world.

Know the thoughts of your heart, and of all who speak and think.

Find the source of life inside you, higher than you, around you. [Find] the beautiful ones alive in this generation in whose midst you are immersed.

The love within you: lift it up to its mighty root, to its beauty of Eden.

Send it spreading out to the entire flood of the soul of the Life of worlds, Whose light is reduced only by incapable human expression.

Gaze at the lights, at what they contain.
Do not let the Names, phrases and letters swallow up your soul.
They have been given over to you.
You have not been given over to them.

Rise up.
Rise up, for you have the power.
You have wings of the spirit, wings of powerful eagles.
Do not deny them, or they will deny you.
Seek them, and you will find them instantly.
Shemonah Kevatzim 1:181

CONTENTS

FROM *OROT HAKODESH*, VOLUME 1

THE ACTIVE WISDOM OF HOLINESS

The wisdom of holiness is more elevated than any other wisdom. That is because it transforms the will and spiritual character of those who study it, bringing them close to that elevated state that constitutes its own most outstanding quality.

This is unlike all secular subjects—which, even when they describe matters that are exalted, beautiful and noble, do not possess the active quality that draws the essential nature of the person studying them to their character. In truth, they have no relationship whatsoever with any of a person's capacities and essential elements, besides his rational ability.

The reason for this is that all holy matters derive from the Source of the life of lives, the Foundation of life, He Who brings everything into being.

Such sanctified content itself has the power to bring into being a multitude of infinite creatures, to "plant the heavens and establish the earth" (*Isaiah* 51:16)—and, how much more, to impress a new stamp in high relief upon the person who studies it.

None of the secular sciences have that ability, for they do not create and forge new matters. Rather, they illustrate and present to the mind's eye that which already exists. Therefore, they cannot transform the person who studies them into a new creature, uprooting him from the essence of his evil traits and placing him in a new state of being, pure and alive in the light of true life, which stands forever and ever.

8:159

HOLY KNOWLEDGE COMES FROM THE SOURCE OF LIFE

The knowledge of the world and reality that comes from the perspective of the mundane does not attain even a ten thousandth—as we can see when we judge truthfully—of the deep knowledge of the world and reality as a whole that comes from the perspective of holiness.

This is because the truth of the absolute reality and being of the whole is present only when we see how the whole comes from the aspect of Divine manifestation, from the aspect of life and existence branching forth from the Source of life and existence.

Everything that is revealed in the form of world and being is merely a sort of weak shadow when contrasted with the pure and mighty existence within the Divine source.

And so the entire richness of a person's knowledge will attain the elevated glory of its greatness only when it is gathered and stored in the source of its being, which is the knowledge of Hashem and His might, the recognition of the whole as seen from the perspective of the Source of the whole.

Then all of the variegated levels of knowledge will be made even. That is because only then, when the supernal height of knowledge is revealed, will the role of knowledge will be appreciated in its true nature.

But when the world is revealed only via its dim shadows—meaning, as long as there is only a vague recognition derived from the aspect of the world's isolated hues and external markings—that leads to a perspective that is as nothing when contrasted with the acquisition of absolute knowledge, which is the knowledge of Hashem, which grows prominent when a person knows the world to be the work of Hashem—a knowledge to which the eyes of all living creatures are raised.

And that absolute knowledge constitutes the whole of a human being, the whole of reality, the whole of that which is recognized and known.

The entire toil of the world, with its elevation level by level, has been established only so that the supernal light of the realm of knowledge will come to be revealed, flowing from its true source.

As for all universal and particular morality, every improvement in the pathways of life—the path of charity and straightness in the life of the individual and of the community—all of that can come to the locus of its perfection only when a person's awareness meets its original being. And that original being constantly rises in accordance with the amount of the revelation of the glory of the light of life within the source of holiness, which is the true radiance, the light of Hashem, Who brings everything into being.

8:153

THE GOODNESS OF THE WISDOM OF HOLINESS

When the wisdom of holiness, in its purity and truth, is revealed in the world, it gives life to all.

It does not impinge on any realm of knowledge, on any greatness and elevation, on any might and glory. Rather, it crowns everything with its yearning for justice, with its goodness and its humility.

All yearnings for justice, in all of their aspects—as applied to the world as a whole and as applied to the individual—find their true entranceway through the wisdom of holiness. And that wisdom helps them realize their endeavors in actuality and in life.

And all good intentions (which are composed of secrets of holiness in Torah, prayer and mitzvos, all together, with all of their details) are pathways through which that self-same supernal light of the wisdom of holiness is revealed, so that this holy manifestation may be brought into the world and satiate the will of every living being, in every-day life and in eternal life.

OH 1:3

THE TRUTH THAT IS DEMANDED BY ALL

The higher a truth is, the simpler it is, and the more is it universally needed.

The narrowness of a person's heart is liable to attempt to dissect truth into parts in order to reduce it. A person is afraid of its greatness, and he thinks that when it is reduced it will be more popular, more universally accessible.

But in truth, with this he makes things more difficult and he withholds from all people that which they most need.

Ultimate truth, Divine truth, is strongly demanded by everyone—and precisely in all of its truthfulness, at the very peak of its light, with its full truth. And precisely because of that, it is fit for everyone: for all flesh, for every creature, for every active being.

A person's knowledge—in the realm of his freedom of choice and in the realm of his will—stands in its central place. It must, even after his great effort to dissect truth, to shorten it in order to reduce it and make it fit for the masses, return to its greatness and purity. "Every created being will know that You made it and every creature will understand that You formed it, and everyone who has a soul in his nostrils will say, 'Hashem, God of Israel, is King, and His sovereignty extends over everything'" (Rosh Hashanah prayerbook).

Fortunate are we, how goodly is our portion, in that we have been chosen for the task of causing the great and simple truth to dwell in the world, the truth upon which the life of every soul depends and which is blended with the creation of the light of the entire world.

We have this ability in our essence—in each individual and in the whole people. It is in the stamp of our genealogy, in the nature of our flesh, in the composition of our land, in the soul of our great forefathers.

"The holy ones who are in the earth and the mighty ones—all of my delight is in them" (*Psalms* 16:3).

"I have planted you as a noble vine stock, entirely a seed of truth" (*Jeremiah* 2:21).

5:15

THE PLAIN OF HALACHAH AND AGGADAH

When we begin to take steps upon the plain of halachah and aggadah, a multitude beyond number of unions and harmonies beyond number is drawn out. The universes of heaven and earth, humanity of the flesh and humanity of ideas, with all the wealth hidden in each of them, are then unified. They bring each other to the wished-for action that leads toward complete growth and perfection.

This connection is nothing less than the revelation of the unity that had been hidden within them from the very beginning.

Whoever has not tasted the flavor of halachah has not tasted the flavor of Torah. And whoever has not tasted the flavor of aggadah has not tasted the flavor of fear of sin.

Torah and fear of sin must always accompany one another. The service of Torah learning must be methodically revealed, in an active form, upon this unifying basis—one whose results are very great.

In truth, aggadah always contains a halachic essence. Similarly, halachah contains an inner agaddic content. In the main, the content of aggadah is found in the qualitative form of halachah. And the content of halachah is found in the quantitative form of aggadah. Even without any particular search or awareness, when we learn halachah, we are touched by its hidden content of aggadah; and, when we learn aggadah, we are touched by the pulse of halachah that is folded into the content of the aggadah.

However, not everyone has a properly keen awareness of these two streams—each of which is constantly filled with the content of the other. An alienation between these worlds, which are in essence so joined and twinned together, leads to an unhealthy separation in the nature of deep study and its broadening. It constricts these two areas—halachic and the aggadic—to a narrow arena.

We must clearly bring forth the meeting of these two forces in a rectified form, when each will make the other s content exceedingly fragrant. Each will profoundly aid the other to bring forth its details and to shine a more brilliant light upon its own general appearance and upon the depth of its own internal logic and what that embraces. The scent of aggadah must make halachah fragrant, in a measure that is well-reasoned and fitting. And aggadah must be given its worth within a framework, with set laws and a clear, defined logic—like the form of a strengthened halachah. With this, the power and freshness of both will be multiplied.

The need that brought the masters of pilpul in previous generations to at times attempt to integrate aggadah and halachah welled forth from this demand for a unification of these forces, which so much act in unison.

We are already called upon to gather together talents and knowledge in order to clarify our learning and all the paths of our lives. In particular, the essence of halachic learning must be broad, composed of the various approaches of the early and later authorities who have grown to be so many over the generations—we very much need that depth and breadth. And we must approach with complete breadth the unity of the contents of halachah and aggadah—which includes the categories of logic and history, ethics and faith, feeling and civility.

And resting upon all of them is a pure phenomenon, one soaked with the dew of the life of the totality of the light of Torah, ready to rest like a beautiful ornament upon all those who learn Torah for its own sake, giving them a special sensitivity and satisfaction of the heart-inspiring joy of Torah.

5:2

YOUR INDEPENDENT INTUITION

It is not the intent of any influence that comes from outside yourself and into your inner being—whether from secular or holy sources—to silence your spirit and mute your independent intuition.

Rather, its intent is to wash you with a flow of light, so that you will absorb it into the essence of who you are.

In this way, and from the midst of this, your independent sense of things will grow ever stronger.

When you are desolated by internal shoddiness, you think that the intention of everything that comes from outside yourself is to abrade your independent sense of reality, to make you crumple, and you totter. You become short-tempered and you cease to grow.

Together, the holy and the secular influence your spirit. When you integrate them, you are enriched.

You must take what is fitting from each of them.

From the holy, take the light of life and an inner character.

From the secular, take the container, the superficial understanding that provides a basis for grasping the content. The secular provides material for analogies and explanations, for contexts of understanding the ways of the world and good character traits.

There is an abundance that is the sense of division between the holy and the secular.

That abundance becomes ever more clear when you gather the wealth of these various sources. It strengthens and illumines your spirit.

At last, you come to the innermost circle of Torah. The diseased cloud within you that hides the Torah begins to glow more and more with the light of Torah. From the fog, lights are revealed in their full beauty.

5:134

THE WELL OF MYSTICAL HINTS

Mystical hints are similar to works of abstract art. Just as abstract art fulfills a certain role in secular matters, these hints fulfill a similar role in matters of holiness.

The more that the well of genius is filled with the liquid of life, the more does it cause the created object to branch out in varied, rich images. If the well is very great, it creates structures that are far from reality and that no eye has seen nor ear heard. It is precisely in these images that the wondrous life based on creation is revealed; they represent the testimony of the soul of their creator.

The more that the great satisfaction of the light and faith-filled life wells forth, so do the mystical hints skip logical steps in an increasingly greater and mightier fashion. Beneath every tendril of these mystical hints are hidden a full wealth and treasure of ethics and faith, beauty of holiness, powerful radiance and Godly, inner trust. These comprise the strength and desire of Israel, the joy of all whose hearts are straight, those who seek God and His strength.

5:119 1:876

PREPARE YOURSELF FOR THE MEASURE OF SILENCE

The entire realm of consciousness, with everything that comes from it, down to the very lowest levels ([in other words], the entirety of existence) shifts between times of silence and times of speech.

When the universe prepares itself to receive a supernal outpouring [from God], everything is still and silent. Then, when those forces that have received God's outpouring pour it forth to those below them, speech begins.

Our [human] reality also shifts in this manner.

When we direct our mind to improving qualities that are below our [spiritual] level, then our consciousness is constricted, and we are active in the world.

But when our supernal attention grows strong, this constricted consciousness can no longer act.

At that time, silence begins to rule.

When you reach this level, the normal activity of consciousness (whether it is dealing with everyday or holy matters) is below you.

You find within yourself a great, unceasing opposition to any activity of consciousness that is rational and structured.

Prepare yourself for the measure of silence. Take heed of the voice from above that brings blessing and good will and spontaneously gives to you.

God's word will come to you. Day to day expresses speech.

8:321, ?

THE TORCH OF IMPECCABLE INTENT

Humanity must develop a great deal before it can realize the great appreciation that the idealism hidden in the depths of the soul has for intent and will. The soul is at all times adorned in a wealth of new colors. These colors display a small part of its treasure and beautiful greatness.

All great, moral actions in this world—whether on a small or on a broad level—are more than small manifestations, tiny sparks of the great torch of impeccable intent.

Intent is everything.
The coming to life of intent is the coming to life of the world.

There is prayer with intent, divine union with intent, mitzvah and obligation with intent, possibility and the breadth of life with intent.

And there is the intent itself. It has an intellectual and moral shape, with its glory and grandeur, its charm and holiness, its unending elevation—its divine heights.

There is the intent that stands out in letters, in names—in which each letter and vowel is a depth and abundance of seas and currents, great and broad channels of life, desire, idealism and wisdom, power and might, emanation and beauty.

And there is the intent that adheres to the holy bodies of pure, ideal human beings. All the joy of their lives is straightness and goodness in action and in morals. This is an intent that is living and fresh. How much light does it shine into the world!

And then the supernal realm of secrets arrives. It connects the intending soul with the wellsprings of the life of ideas, with the root of their root.

Then an infinite light, the light of the living God, spills forth, gushing in every syllable and action.

Intent is the birth of action.

Within the supernal intent and the intent that is filled with Divine life are included every thought of peace and every thought of the war for justice and right, every victory of wisdom and of a good and pleasant order.

Every rectification of the world is included within it.

Orot Hakodesh I, pp. 124-25

THE APPEARANCE OF CREATIVITY

Our spirit places within us the image of its creations. We recognize that angel, filled with life, who sits upon the birth stool, bringing forth its works. That angel is flying in the heights, approaching us, appearing to our souls—behold, it comes!

We welcome that angel with great peace and joy. The angel appreciates our affection in the most refined, pure, alive and strong manner—more than we ourselves, encased in physicality, can appreciate it.

And then, we have finished the work of creation—or it has suddenly, unfinished, ceased. Lift your eyes upon the angel—yet it is not there. The cherub has taken flight and risen to the heights—and our spirit is diminished.

We then concern ourselves with Torah and wisdom, good deeds and character improvement, in order to gain connection to our holy angels, in order to strengthen our own might with the great power of the gracious God, Who appears to us in His light and salvation.

A host of different states mingles within us: strength and weakness meet, love and abhorrence mix, trust and fear act as one, light and darkness are in confusion. All this results from the paucity of our purification.

Let us rise higher. The return to Godliness shall grow and rise with mighty strength; the will shall rise in its holy exaltation. We ascend beyond the flesh and its pollutions, we ascend beyond the falsehood and seduction of our environment. In truth, we cleave to truth; the light waxes stronger, and life is exalted.

Orot Hakodesh I, p. 167

THE CREATIVE SOUL

It is impossible to interrupt the creativity of a person whose soul by its nature creates unceasingly.

When one is oppressed by spiritual malaise, this is only because one believes creativity to be a burden. But the more one descends to its secret, the more does one comes to realize that it is not burdensome or wearisome. One imitates one's Maker: the Holy One, blessed be He, did not create His world with toil and trouble; He perfected it without fatigue and exhaustion, but with the means of a letter that has no weight and suffers no weariness.

The true tzaddikim, who are supernal, holy beings, in their essence rise beyond all toil and fatigue.

They would be satisfied with all toil and trouble, all suffering and difficulty, all sacrifice and backbreaking labor, only to do the will of the living God and King of the world, the Creator of their souls, the King of Israel and its Redeemer, the Master of all creatures and God of all spirits. But despite their willingness, they are filled with comfort and peace; the flow of pleasures flows constantly in their holy souls. A breath of richness and abundance penetrates into their breath, spirit and body, all their inner being, bones and flesh. From the midst of the pleasure of this supernal glory, they take pleasure in a supernal fear and love in their service, in all the breaths of their spirit, and in all their lives and movements—theirs is entirely a supernal, Godly service, with no interruption, no ceasing, whatsoever.

The flow of this well of mindfulness and emotion constantly pours within them from all sides. All that they pay heed to, hear, feel physically and feel emotionally—speaks glory; speaks, "Holy, holy, holy is the Lord of Hosts, the earth is filled with His glory"; speaks peace and blessing to every living thing, to all flesh. "The heavens and earth, with all that moves upon them, will praise Him." The freedom of the creation and its blessings gain breadth in their mind and heart.

At every moment, new worlds are born, formed and exist. The worlds that were already created are elevated to a new form that is supernal, holy, precious, and beautiful. These worlds are renewed in every expression and word, in a flow of forms that are new and ultra-new, that rise like waves, like a host of great breakers.

None is tired, none stumbles; there is no toil or weariness—rather, comfort and joy. "I will rejoice in Hashem, I will have joy in the God of my salvation."

But if these tzaddikim, these supernal holy ones, do not believe in themselves, if they do not pay attention to the voice of the shofar of supernal freedom that calls to them, then a profusion of waters will plummet upon them and endanger their lives; they shall be submerged in the muddy depths, until they recognize their greatness and beauty, their glow and holiness.

Then, in place of the pressure toward toil and depression that rests upon them—which would desecrate the name of their God—they will, with strength and joy in its place, rise to freedom and pleasure. They will know how to unite all the flames of their ardor, all their movements—and not only their own but also of those who join their circle, of whoever comes in contact with them and stands before them in the shared vision with a complete unity, with the brilliant, living and precious light that sparks forth from the glow of the Almighty, Whose glory fills the world, Whose eminence and beauty rests upon all His pious ones.

Orot Hakodesh I, pp. 168-69

THE FLOW OF THE SOUL'S CREATIVITY

Those who possess great souls live precisely from within their wellspring. These wise, creative people, to whom the new is the foundation of their life, recognize only in the pouring forth of newness (which ceaselessly streams before their spiritual sight) the constant spreading forth of their caliber and the intensification of their spiritual strengths. They recognize the soul in the depth of its primal being: how it constantly pours forth its cataracts.

With no less actuality than a shining body that unceasingly radiates light, so does the soul—which experiences recognition and desire, feeling and visualization—pour forth the rays of its spiritual, living light. This stream pours forth ever more strongly, creates ever more strongly. No amount of pages will suffice to explain the vision of any period of this streaming forth of the soul in even the smallest of people. Thus does this wealth grow until it comes to be within the exalted thinkers, the greatest creators: to such a wondrous level that the masses are astonished at the illuminations revealed in the fruit of their creations.

And this is so even though the portion that is revealed is by necessity the lowest level of the essence of creation. As for the essence of the creation in its hidden aspect: wondrous are its acts, and its streams, which are the streams of the mind, rush forth. It does not allow us to grasp the inner essence, the quality and the details of these pouring streams.

The most worthy talent is the penetration into the depth of our essential being. Yet how trivial is the work of that talent and how much does it infect the exalted heights with toil and weariness of soul. To the degree that one recognizes this and recognizes how much that penetration must grow aware of the demand of the inner Edenic quietude—to that measure will grow the exalted being within creativeness. Then sparks of holiness will begin to shoot forth upon all of life and its spiritual ramifications.

At every moment, even the most infinitesimal, we create—whether knowingly or unknowingly—a profusion of endless creations. If we only teach ourselves to feel them, to bring them into the realm of our conscious recognition, to habituate ourselves to convey them into the framework of expressions that are fit for them, their beauty and glory will be revealed. Their action will be revealed before all of life.

The eternal truths will flow from the wellspring of life, from the source of the soul that does not know of any empty matters or falsehood. That soul is carved from the torch of truth; whatever streams from its light will be only truth and righteousness forever.

Orot Hakodesh I, pp. 170-71

ILLUMINATION OF THE SOUL

As long as a person must wait for particular periods of time for the spirit of creativity to occur to him—at which opportunity he will generate ideas, contemplate them, express them and sing them—this is a sign that the light of his soul has not rested upon him.

The soul sings constantly, clothed in strength and beauty, surrounded by supernal sweetness. One must rise to the heights and meet one's soul. One must recognize its spiritual progress, the rustle of its wings filled with a glory of the holy of holies; one must be constantly ready to listen to the secret of its holy speech. Then one will know that it is not at some particular time or period that the soul generates wisdom and expression, song and holy speech, but rather that at every moment and every hour it pours forth rivers and streams of milk and honey.

The river that flows from the soul comprises the treasuries of holiness, the wellsprings of understanding and the hidden sources of good wisdom. "New in the morning, great is Your faithfulness."

With an inner gaze into the depths of the soul, we see that the active, constant power of true, supernal life does not cease working for even a moment. That power races and returns like the lightning in Ezekiel's vision; its work is the service of the holy seraphim; it constantly bursts forth in joy and song, telling the glory of God.

The essential "I" of the person who possesses this supernal soul is stupendous. But when the mighty faith is diminished by that "I," it goes in mourning, and that person is desolate. And with him, the radiance of the entire world is diminished.

But when he returns in a supernal manner, when the glory of faith with its supernal powers (which pulse within him constantly without fail) returns to him, then his soul will live and shine forth. All the worlds that are at his feet and proceed with him will be filled with radiance and illumination.

Orot Hakodesh I, pp. 172-73

CONSTANT SELF-REVELATION

Do not oppose the essential soul when it reveals itself. That self-revelation is constant. Even when the thickest clouds mask the soul's brilliant light, it shines with all its power. It carries the world and every human being to the goal of his fulfillment—a goal that transcends all definitions.

The soul speaks without speaking. It acts without acting. With it alone do we ascend those steps to which we are impelled by the impulse of that which is truly life, in its most profound mysteries. "Then shall you rejoice in God."

This is the secret of thirst and the mystery of its quenching.

Orot Hakodesh I, p. 173

HEEDING THE VISION

We heed the call of the holy discourse that descends from the heights. We gather the impressions that spark like lightning, that are revealed from the heights of the soul, from its roots.

Every revealed vision is a voice that calls from the heights: from the source of knowledge, from the treasury of life within the soul of the Life of all worlds. It is revealed to each individual in accordance with the purity of his ascent, the purification of who he is in essence. To the degree that the sins that divide one from one's Maker, the Maker of all, are removed, so does the voice go forth from the source of supernal oneness with the greatest and truest revelation.

Whatever one creates, whether physical or spiritual, must be properly prepared and purified. The holy yearning for Godly exaltedness in the beauty of its glory (clothed within the perfect robe of ethics, in all walks of life) must go forth, creating its own path.

Then, the dividing walls flee. A direct light and a direct voice arrive, imbued with the treasury of life and the wisdom of truth.

The ear hears and the eye sees. God has made them both.

Orot Hakodesh I, p. 174

THE INNER SPARK

The very essence of the soul, which expresses and experiences the true, spiritual life, requires complete inner freedom. This freedom is its life.

This freedom comes to the soul from the midst of its essential thought, its inner spark. One's learning and contemplation cause this spark to continually flame. But really, this independent spark is the basis of idea and thought. If room is not provided for the independent spark with its light to appear, then whatever comes to it from without will be of no avail

This spark must be guarded in its purity. Then the inner thought—in the depth of its truth, in its greatness and exaltedness—will awake.

Then this holy spark will not be extinguished because of any learning and any contemplation.

The internal unity of the soul in the core of itself represents the supernal greatness of the illuminated, Divine seed—"light is sown for the righteous." From this seed, the fruit of the tree of life shall sprout and blossom.

Orot Hakodesh I, p. 175

THE LIBERATED GAZE

The more you perceive your spiritual state,
The more will you realize that all of your images
Can be limitless.
Your ability to visualize
Can be fully attained.

So visualize, to whatever degree,
Greatness and strength.
Still, you will attain less
Than a drop from the ocean
Of what can be grown and ennobled.

Your liberated gaze,
Touched with the joy of refined imagination,
Might satisfy you.
That still won't approach
The smallest degree
Of the true state of Eden
Within all of existence—
All of which reveals supernal joy:
That Eden of the Creator of all worlds.
Orot Hakodesh I, p. 176

THE FREEDOM OF INNER CREATIVITY

Spiritual creation is free. It doesn't deal with any superficial influence. It creates in accordance with the journey of its spirit to the core. To the degree that its essential faith grows, so does it rise to the heights of truth.

On the other hand, falsehood and the evil attached to it come only from a superficial influence. This influence affects spiritual creativity like a scab. It commands spiritual creativity to speak with the power of falseness, and not according to its own spirit. "He has chosen to follow the command" (Hosea 5:11)—the command (the sages say) of idolatry.

Orot Hakodesh I, p. 176

BREADTH OF THOUGHT

When your soul is creative,
You must create
Ideas and thoughts.
You cannot restrict yourself
To superficial learning.
The flame of your soul spontaneously rises.
You cannot restrict its progress.

Breadth of thought
Is the unceasing demand
That every creative person
Requires of himself.

Superficial learning can restrict thought
And muddle it at birth.
Constant learning
With superficial constancy
Increases the malady
Of narrow-mindedness.

With all our strength,
We must be redeemed from that.
We must deliver our soul
From the oppression of its straits.
We must deliver it from Egypt,
From the house of slavery.
Orot Hakodesh I, p. 177

THE AWARENESS OF POETRY AND BEAUTY

Each new Torah insight
Must basically be ideal:
Based
On the depth of rectitude in our ethical being;
On the depth of holiness in our faithful being;
On the depth of expression in our intellectual being;
Enveloped in the awareness of poetry and beauty
In our creative being.
Orot Hakodesh I, p. 178

LIGHTS, NEW AND ALIVE

Attaining understanding from your own consciousness is the highest point of spiritual elevation.

That which you learn, you grasp from without, and it descends in its character. How different this is from the expression that rises from the midst of your soul!

That which you learn is at best a profound idea teaching you to draw forth what is hidden in your heart, in the depths of your soul: the essence of what you can comprehend from your consciousness.

Your consciousness streams forth constantly, creative and active.

The supernal creative person does not create but only duplicates. He draws lights, new and alive, from a supernal source to where they have never been—from a place the eagle has not known, where no eye has gazed, no man has passed, none has dwelled.

When such personal greatness is revealed, one's ear is faithful; one's heart hearkens and says nothing that it has not heard from its teachers, the true, righteous prophets, whose mouths are true with the word of God.

Orot Hakodesh I, p. 178

THE WORLD OF HUMANITY

Spiritual idealism knows nothing of quantitative separation. It recognizes only inclusivity and unity. It surveys particulars only as being a factor within the totality. Therefore, it can only recognize an all-inclusive goodness. And it can only recognize evil when it is all-inclusive. And because an all-inclusive evil does not exist at all, and all-inclusiveness proceeds in relation to the manifestations in the form of time, for idealism does not considers and is connected to its unique point, but with its entire great outpouring, as a result, it comes to recognize that there is no universality to the existence of evil. Rather, all is goodness. "And God saw everything He had made, and behold, it was very good."

Physical mass creates a separation between existing objects and, automatically, their opposing natures.

As long as an awareness of good and evil exists, you do not have to connect your nature to this state of being: "he may not eat from the tree of knowledge of good and evil." Only the tree of life, which is all good, is prepared for you. Also prepared for you is: "Eat from the tree of knowledge of good and evil"—after you pass the many tests that you must go through, when your pollution is continuously cleansed, so that you are completely purified and your character traits are rectified, and the awareness of the tree of life again connects with you. Then the tree of knowledge of good and evil turns into a tree filled entirely with life and goodness.

There is no generation in which this great labor, clarifying awareness and the will in order to burn evil from its existence, will be completed. This is the foundation and maintenance of the world. "Say to the tzaddik that it is good." The world is renewed when the Torah is renewed. A revelation that comes in a limited form is a reduced condensation with no measure or value at all, after the spiritual and mighty waves have already gushed and gone by, descended from world to world, contracted again and again, until they finally appeared to us in the form of some revelation.

In its root, revelation is not individual, intellectual illumination, but global: the revelation of a new heavens, or a new earth—depending on what you dealt with, its worth and its content.

The same greatness that spreads through the soul, whose incandescence breaks down and weakens the frame of the letters, is the greatness that includes within its hiddenness all the details of the lights that illumine the letters.

To reveal the letters and their details, pray and direct your heart to our Father in heaven, Who is all-powerful, Who merges them together, the great and the small: "He sits on His throne, and gazes down on heaven and earth." From the supernal light of true prayer, the prayer of the righteous, a great light emerges from the region of supernal equality, where no light pushes light aside, but each strengthens and illumines the other. This light, this dew of desire, causes all the letters, with their vowels and their smallest details, to sprout from that supernal illumination itself.

Orot Hakodesh I, p. 179

THE LIGHT OF OUR IMAGINATION

All truth and greatness exist in the treasure-house of imagination. It gradually becomes successively refined, as it passes through a number of conduits of the intellect, which reduce and purify it.

We are summoned to appear in the light of our imagination, in the full splendor of its life-force, in the complete, precious, beautiful greatness of its holiness, on the world plane. There, all of humanity will gaze toward us and stream toward us.

Our rational intellect is no more than a small student who partially explains all the light of life that rests within the treasure house of our rich, holy imagination—which lives on an exalted plane of life, which influences realistic existence with the solid essence of its being.

Let us acknowledge the greatness of strength of life of our supernal imagination, which transcends all arid straits and limitations that are part of the conditions of an impoverished, dry existence.

With the strength of imagination, suffused with the richness of life, we rise higher and higher. Imagination unites with supernal intellect—to which the name "intellect" is not really fitting, because it is so great and brilliant.

Guard the hidden treasure, the nameless wisdom, the divine lightning flash, which blazes and sparkles from one end of the world to the other; the treasure in the ways of life that the mouth of God has spoken so that He may teach them to us on the paths of faith and education, higher than the heavens.

These ways of life rise, ever higher and higher, and they descend in the strength of their selflessness to inherit the land, to guide the masses of the nation, to revive the dead, to support the humble, to beautify and glorify all those who walk in darkness.

Return, come. Return and live. Be a nation. Be a holy people and a supernal nation, as you were meant to be from the very beginning.

Find for yourself the depth of the greatness of who you are. Rise to your own great strength.

Do not fear the criticism of man. Do not be upset by the dreams of the foolish. Raise the supernal banner over everything, the banner that shall be flourished by the nation chosen by God, the God of the world.

Orot Hakodesh I, p. 223

THE QUALITIES OF IMAGINATION

In imagination, there exist qualities that do not exist in intellect.

Imagination brings to life within us the world in its spiritual state. Automatically, it perfects our spiritual quality. (However, when it grows stronger, it adulterates the form of the world of action.)

Cultural experiments have brought about a great deal of enrichment in the realm of the physical sciences, as well as the spiritual sciences that are based on the physical sciences.

But at the same time, the world of imagination and all the greatness of life within it have degenerated steeply.

And so, present-day humanity is puny in relation to early mankind, particularly in relation to those great people whose imagination grew and acquired those portions it needed from this-worldly intellect.

Therefore, we justifiably still proclaim, even after the great development of the modern sciences: "If the first generations were like angels, we are like human beings. And if they were like human beings, we are like donkeys."

Orot Hakodesh I, p. 225

IN THE SEEDBED OF IMAGINATION

In the seedbed of imagination lie the beginnings of intellectual awareness—in a constricted form.

This form shines more and more, constantly spreading and developing. At last, from the clouds of imagination comes forth a content that is wise and refined.

Intellectual awareness spreads in truth over all existence: over nature and its ramifications, as well as the many components that surround nature from without.

The same process applies to the seed of imagination, which spreads across all the length, width, depth, and height within existence.

The heights of wisdom are at last revealed in a revelation that is consecrated in a manner appropriate to each of its levels. It is crowned in the kingdom of action, in the actions of being as they connect, with many and various bonds, to their cause.

And in parallel, the same process occurs in imagination.

From the height of levels, the content plunges into the steep depth.

It proceeds from the beginning of prophecy and the divine, supernal illumination in the glory of holiness to the lowliness of charisma, with its gestures and illusions. It proceeds from the beginning of cerebral clarity, an emanation of exceedingly fine purity, to the most confused delusions of imagination.

Through all of these proceeds one line, divided into its levels.

Those who gaze from the crown of the tree penetrate all the depths.

There is neither darkness nor shadow of death, for Sheol and Destruction are in the presence of God.

And in the spirit of man, all is intertwined and connected. He must elevate all and beautify it, in order to bring the vessel forth to its Maker.

Orot Hakodesh I, p. 229

TWO EXTREMES OF SLEEP

Sleep—and, generally, the natural character of the night, which causes sleep and which is appropriate for sleep—influences the aspects of life within us in two separate directions.

Our higher, spiritual aspect can rise very high. Our imagination is freed from the framework of the senses. If it is constantly connected to the intellect and to a supernal, holy desire, it can visualize and imagine, gaze and recognize those things it will not sense when we are awake.

On the other hand, the power of life within our body now lacks its connection to our spiritual aspect. That power acts alone, expressing its natural tendencies in a dark, cloudy form.

To these two points, archetypes cling. Pure lights cling to our supernal soul from a higher illumination. On the other hand, darkness, the desiccation of pollution and gross negative energies cling to the vital spirit, from the dark muck that had been lying within ourselves, that now bubbles up in the mud of a life limited to the physical.

Every morning, we deal with both these energies in serving God. We purify our vital spirit, and we connect ourselves to the lights that have been added to our supernal human soul.

Once again, we fuse the two polarities in felicitous harmony.

Orot Hakodesh I, p. 230

THE DISTANT GAZE

Imagination sends the rays of its brilliance out to the distance, to give image constantly to that which is external to the essence of the thinker; and the intellect circles the central point in the soul of life, and images the existence deep within it.

And in accordance with this, imagination is necessary for the intellect that it may be helped by it for the distant gaze; and the intellect helps and supports the imagination to explain to it how great is the possession that is stored deep within it.

Orot Hakodesh I, p. 238

THE HEART OF THE WISE MAN KNOWS

Feeling is swifter than intellect. In feeling, the word "God" is filled with fecundity and reality even before the smallest fraction of all the multitude of enigmas concealed with it is deciphered.

But this is not the case with intellect. Intellect requires toil. Without study and inquiry, one will find nothing.

If feeling is exchanged for intellect, if one will desire to engage one's intellect without spiritual labor, in order to enjoy the benefit of what is already prepared—as it is possible to do in feeling—one's world will swiftly grow dark. Tangled thorns will flourish in one's spiritual portion, one will constantly be entangled, and one's spiritual path will be filled with stumbling blocks.

"There is a time and judgement that the heart of the wise man knows." And that is: to enter the palace of feeling in its fullness, to take pleasure in its sweet things, and to allow the portion of the intellect to engage in its toil. Then the knowledge of God will enter one's heart in its most desirable form.

Orot Hakodesh I, p. 251

THE LIFE-FORCE OF ALL SPECIES

We find wondrous abilities in animals that at times astonish us. We can reproduce these only after great and long study. Even then, however, we can only approximate those achievements.

What gives these animals their abilities? The lights of the life-force of all species are fragments of a great, supernal soul filled with wisdom and ability, which has been divided into many branches. The glow of this great soul, which contains wondrous wisdom and ability, shines upon each branch in a minute amount—like a drop of water from the sea.

Still, because the point comes from the all-encompassing basis of wisdom and an ability that is mighty and exalted, its essential impression can never be eradicated. The impression brings forth its ability in accordance with the profound greatness of that wisdom; in accordance with the measure that [the wisdom] had had when it had been enclosed and connected—with a connection of a perfect life—to its perfect source; when [the wisdom] had been the content of the crown of wisdom, arranged precisely by the Supernal Consciousness.

Orot Hakodesh I, p. 358

FROM *OROT HAKODESH*, VOLUME 2

TOGETHER, THEY REVEL

When we learn simple matters in Torah, we should be aware of how the supernal light descends in a wondrous form, until it is well-established in this world of action. We should broaden our heart in regard to this great preciousness and the strength of this life-force, which flows from the source of the Holy of Holies, and which is given fullness from the sanctified path of the light of Israel in all the world.

Know clearly that this light, which is so constricted within words and letters, within customs, within actions, within laws, within the tools of logical analysis and reasoning, meets with the supernal light that is elevated above all these. It is cleansed within it.

And together, they revel.

And the light of the Life of the worlds is filled with great radiance and pleasure because of that continuous encounter, which is brought about by the strength of a person learning Torah for its own sake, making peace in the realms above and the realms below.

Orot Hakodesh, II, p. 3

LIMITING GOODNESS WITH GOODNESS

Those who have great souls cannot be separated from the most encompassing inclusiveness. All of their desire and ideal is, constantly, the good of the entire universe in its full breadth, height and depth. This entirety is filled with infinite details of individuals and societies. It is crowned to the degree that it is filled with the perfection of its individual members and its groups, small and great, which complete it.

Supernal inclusiveness, which perfects all, is found within the movement toward knowledge and love of God. That movement emanates automatically from the inclusiveness, in accordance with what that movement has acquired and its wealth.

The knowledge of God that comes through great love must be filled with its own true light, in accordance with what each individual soul can bear and receive. The absolute light of that knowledge of God illumines the universal love: the love of all universes, all created beings, and the entire realm of life and its existence.

The love of all existence fills the heart of those who are good: the pious among all creatures and among humanity. They look forward to the happiness of all. They hope for the light and joy of all. They draw the love of all existence—which contains the full spectrum of the multiplicity of its creations—from the supernal love of God, from the love of the total and complete perfection of God, Who is the Cause of all, Who brings all into being and gives life to all.

Love descends from the world of Emanation to the world of Creation by being divided into many details, into contradictions and opposites. This fulfills the purpose of constriction, the compression of value and love, into individual details, each for the sake of another detail; into many details, each for the sake of many others; and to details in general because of the complete entirety that they comprise.

The shining lens of love stands at the height of the world, in the world of divinity, in a place where there are no contradictions, borders and oppositions—only satisfaction, goodness, and infinite breadth. The offspring of that shining lens of love is eternal love. When eternal love draws sustenance from the shining lens of love, it attains a great deal of its nature. In its descent, it cannot bear any stinginess or jealousy. When it is forced to constrict itself, it constricts love with love; it limits goodness with goodness.

When those who are suffused with love see the world, and in particular, when they see living beings involved in bickering, hatred, persecution and quarreling, they immediately yearn that they and their lives may be partners with desires that bring about the joining together of life and its unity, perfection and tranquility. They feel and know that the closeness of God for which they yearn with the fullness of their soul only functions to bring them to a unification with inclusiveness and for the sake of that inclusiveness.

When they come to the strata of mankind and find factions of nations, religions, sects and opposing ideals, they strive with all their strength to encompass all of it, to connect and to unify. With the healthy spiritual sense of their pure soul, which rises and flies to the Godly heights above all constrictions, they recognize that all details must be full, that the best societal forms must be elevated and must enter with all the satisfaction of their details into the light of a perfected life. They desire that every detail will be guarded and elevated, and the complete entirety united and filled with peace.

When they come to their own nation, their heart is connected with all the depth of their life with the nation's happiness, endurance and elevation. Yet still, they find it divided and split, divided into various parties. They cannot effect a complete unity within any particular party. Rather, they desire to unite with the entire nation, totally and entirely, in all its fullness and goodness.

Orot Hakodesh II, pp. 242-43

A UNION OF STRENGTH AND BEAUTY

A person stands and wonders: What need is there for the profusion of such a variety of creatures? And he fails to understand how they all constitute one great entity.

The slumbering life that exists within inanimate matter marks the beginning of a lightning flash that shines continuously within the vegetative world, splitting into tens of thousands of rays, each unique and individual. These arrive at the sanctuary of life, and there they sparkle joyously; they rise to the height of the crown of the universe's creatures: man. The entirety of the quality of man's life, its streaming illuminations, the constant rising of his spirit—these are merely great ocean waves flowing back and forth, impelled by all the movements of life within existence: from the smallest particle of life to the greatest, from inanimate matter to human being.

If you are astonished at how it is that you are able to speak, hear, smell, feel, see, understand and have emotions, consider that all of life, and all that precedes it, causes all of your existence to flow upon you.

Not even the smallest point is superfluous. Everything is necessary; everything serves its purpose. You [exist] in all that is below you, and you are tied to and rise with all that is higher than you.

Animals, who do not have great intellectual expression, possess an earthy, strong drive. [This drive is] somewhat weakened by its freshness and strength of existence, which is caused by the pressure of its activity. [That in turn is] due to the ideal core of will that has entered into [that drive]. [The animal] draws its complete strength from its connection with the vegetative world, which does not have even that slight disturbance of the revelation of life.

In turn, vegetation, with all its healthy, unwavering [life force], suffers from [its possession of] movement and a limited imaginative faculty. It is healed from its weakness by being connected to the inanimate world, which has a spirit of permanence and constant, solid strength.

The peak of life arises within man. [But it] is very much weakened by the freedom that characterizes [his] will. [In turn,] it attains its strength by being connected to the more corporeal world of life.

The various strata of mankind are linked by this law as well. The ideal side [of man] stands ready to collapse from the weakness that resides within refinement. But it attains a [firm] stance by being based on the tangible aspect of reality.

And thus, all creatures in the world constitute one entity. Nations and parties, people of different opinions and temperament, together build a world that is full: filled with a union of strength and beauty.

Orot Hakodesh II, p. 361

WITH THE SPIRIT OF ALL CREATION

Our temporary existence is only one spark of our eternal existence, the glory of ever-lasting life. There is only one way to bring forth the wealth of goodness concealed within our this-worldly life: and that is our connection to our eternal life.

This is an inner understanding that dwells within the spirit of all creation. All the spiritual battles in the world cannot dislodge it. All they do is prepare the way before it. Even those forces that oppose this understanding ultimately, in the depths of truth, support it.

A life of true civility and culture is based solidly on one's connection to eternity.

The yearning for the glory of that eternity overwhelms death. It wipes the tear from every eye.

Orot Hakodesh II, p. 377

DEATH IS A FALSE PHENOMENON

Death is a false phenomenon. What makes death unclean is that it spreads an aura of falsehood. Actually, what people call death is the opposite: an ascent into an even greater and more real life.

We are plunged into the depths of small-mindedness. What has placed us here? Our physical and emotional drives. These drives, gazing upon this ascent into life, interpret it as a dreadful, black phenomenon that they label: death.

In their purity, the cohanim must shield themselves from this falsehood. The only way to escape while this false consciousness lays spread across the earth is to avert one's eyes from any sights that cause one's soul to err. That is why the cohanim are commanded to avoid the vicinity of any dead person—for in their human apprehension of death, this falsehood, they are defiled.

Orot Hakodesh II, p. 380

WE ARE CONSOLED FOR THE DUST AND ASHES

When we gaze at that within creation which our senses can perceive, we view it as one organic being. We see that its parts are connected and integrated: every plant and every animal.

As for humanity: we see how those highest parts within us, which carry a splendor of all-inclusive, ideal awareness, rely in their nature, being and existence on particular, primitive, mean components that we sometimes view with revulsion.

The same dynamic applies universally to inter-relationship.

When we gaze clearly, we clearly see with an individual precision. Even where our eye cannot penetrate, we discern with a clear understanding and a comprehension that is spiritual and profound: how all components of existence are interdependent.

The deepest depths and the highest mountains are inter-related. They are integrated with each other.

This awareness constantly makes us recognize that only because of the dark and unsightly lower states of being do the highest states of being, honorable and bright, come forth and climb to the zenith of their splendor.

Then integration and unity constantly increase within us.

From the world of the tangible, we move to the world of the non-material, to the thoughts and schemes of man, to the avenues of various cultures, faiths and systems.

And we are repelled, seeing how evil and foolishness have ruled and continue to rule in the paths of the human heart: in customs, opinions, beliefs, in how people live—privately and socially. We look at the abominations justified by faith, at all the sacrifices of humanity to idolatry, at all the victims of vile custom and at all the evils, degradations, weakness and darkness that have gained broad acceptance.

On the other hand, we see flashes: the crown of grace of humanity's intelligence and virtue, the wisdom of the wise, the courage of the mighty, the flaming holy light of a pure and elevated faith, the ideals and hopes for the great future, and pillars of light that pervade the present.

Seeing both of these, we immediately realize: all of this, all this non-material vision constitutes one world. It too has an organic content. It too, with the entire splendor of its soul, with the lightning flash of its holy spirit and the might of the God of gods within it, relies upon its base, upon its cellar. If not for the trash within the spirit of man, the fruit of our understanding—which gives joy to God and man—would not blossom.

Then immediately, we are consoled for the dust and ashes. We lovingly accept the profound wisdom of the universal Architect, the Creator of all being, the God of all spirits, the Master of all souls, Who gives a soul to the people of the land and a spirit to those who walk upon it—so that from His goodness we may all draw goodness.

Ever more strongly, we are girded with holiness and might. We begin to recognize our lowliness and greatness—simultaneously.

We take pleasure in the flowers of grace and beauty that have blossomed upon the flower beds of human history. In this, we recognize something more exalted, something unendingly greater.

We are all permeated with the yearning of song, we are all filled with might: to walk upright upon the road of light, to know the greatness within the ultimate harvest of the spirit, where all goodness and virtue, all light and freedom blossom.

We take the fruit of faith in its purity, in its first-born state, to the degree that we can reach it, in accordance with our straight path of understanding. And as for whatever sparkles within us beyond the power of our mind, we know with faith that from the very heights, God guards.

We are resolved to teach our upright wisdom. We are filled with the excellence of that divine greatness which we know as an inheritance from the early masters, from the teachings of the holy assemblies.

"Who is like You, mighty God, surrounded by Your faithfulness?" (Psalms 89:9).

Orot Hakodesh II, pp. 417-18

FINDING ONESELF

Each individual finds himself within himself.
Then he finds himself within his surroundings:
His friends, community and people.

The community finds itself within itself.
Then it finds itself within all humanity.

Humanity finds itself within itself—at least, at first.
Then it finds itself within the world.

The world finds itself within itself.
Then it finds itself within all the worlds surrounding it.

The entirety of universal encompassing finds itself within itself.
Then it finds itself within the all-inclusive, supernal classification of all concepts of universe.

The concept of universe finds itself within itself.
Then it finds itself within the full treasury, the supernal light, the multitude of life as well as the source of its days, and in the divine illumination.

All of these recognitions fuse together.
They become one unit, whose inclusiveness is infinitely glorious, whose particular nature is strong, flawless, whole and outstanding—
Endless and perpetual.

The flow of life flows ever more strongly
And the light of holiness grows ever more strongly.
"The singers and flute-players [proclaim] together:
All of my wellsprings are within you, [Zion]!" (Psalms 87:7).
Orot Hakodesh II, p. 447

THE SUPERFICIAL AND THE PROFOUND

There are two ways of looking at the world: the viewpoint of unity and the viewpoint of separation.

The viewpoint of unity looks at the entire vista of individuals separated from each other as no more than an error of the senses and a lack of illumination. But the truth of reality is simply one great unity. The many, variegated beings are merely particular expressions—different limbs, various colors and hues—of that one, unified uniqueness.

In this viewpoint of unity, you look upon the whole. Then, automatically, an accounting of goodness emerges. Everything together is certainly good—with an ultimate goodness—much better because of the revelation of its evil parts than if those limbs, those means of expression, had been lacking.

To the degree that this unifying recognition grows deeper and stronger, so is its truth revealed in its penetration to the depths, in its rule over life.

All feelings proceed in accordance with the nature of that unifying recognition. Everything is felt with the feeling of goodness.

Then goodness grows stronger—goodness upon goodness. Joy rises above joy; life more glorious upon life.

The more that this unifying view strikes deep roots, the more does it bring actualized goodness into the world: life and peace.

Opposing this supernal viewpoint is the separating viewpoint, which sees a variegated reality as the true vision, and claims the foreignness of all details to each other as a true recognition.

The senses and every superficial awareness aid in this. In accordance with this, life grows progressively more corporeal. The greater its effects, so do darkness and evil increase.

There is no end to the depth of war between these two points of view: the superficial and the profound.

But all the avenues of cause in the world proceed to one point, bringing into actuality the rule of the unified viewpoint in all worlds, subjugating the viewpoint of separation to itself.

***

The faith in divine unity is the soul, carrying within itself all the treasure of life, all the inner possessions in which the treasure of all the worlds is stored.

***

Political leaders and all communal leaders are rooted in the foundation of the viewpoint of separation, in the power of illusion that displays reality in its divided state.

The world is not yet fit for a leadership from the viewpoint of unity, in its purity.

***

The quality of light of the Messiah, the place of the throne of God in the world—"this is his name that he will be called:

The Lord-is-our-Righteous-One (Jeremiah 23:6)"—is built upon the foundation of the viewpoint of actual unity, growing so strong that it penetrates all particulars and all causes.

***

It is necessary that the viewpoint of unity be hidden.

Because of all the unity in existence, because everything is in truth complete goodness from the aspect of its unity, that goodness of constant elevation is not nullified. That constant elevation is marked by the refinement of every particular matter and its elevation.

However, when this illumination of delight is revealed, the pressure and refinement that raise each particular and return every evil to goodness do not grow sufficiently strong.

Therefore, it is the hidden nature of the united light that sends forth the inner uniqueness, the essential nature of the unifying light, to the depths of separation. These are the birth pangs and torments that cause the supernal light to be revealed.

The sparks of holiness scattered in the depths of darkness join together, one by one, because of the descent of the supernal, unified light into the depths of hiddenness of the viewpoint of separation.

***

This miracle of the revelation of light of the life of unity in the individual and in the world, with the processes of its ethical nature and its deepest longings—which envelop and permeate everything—is alive. It is alive within Israel.

"His people Israel lives and exists forever."

"The name of the Lord, God of the world is called upon him."

"In the light of His countenance does he walk."

"The Lord his God is with him, and the friendship of the king with him."

Orot Hakodesh II, pp. 456-58

THE RETURN TO NATURE

There are three levels upon which the individual and collective perfection of Israel must be based. These are the return to nature, to the ethics of humanity and to the foundation of the nation. Supernal holiness rests only upon these three.

The highest divine service is that which is connected directly to nature. This supernal holiness was polluted by the human defilement that destroyed the service of nature, making it a monster of idolatry instead of a firm foundation for supernal idealism.

The lofty luminosity of Adam incorporates a supernal quality that rises higher than the clear lens of prophecy that was attained by our teacher, Moses. "To work and guard" the garden of Eden is the radiance of supernal life: to eat of the tree of life and know nothing at all of any evil, because it is completely impossible that there should exist in the physical and spiritual world— which is so perfect, which is the work of the hands of the Creator of everything—anything evil. Everything in its season and its time is solely good. "God made man straight."

Engaging in "the chapter of song" is the foundation of the return to nature. This is a low return that is high, that rises beyond all national jealousy, solely lifting man to become an elevated brother to his other brothers: the creations of the Almighty, who all know their Maker and take pleasure in the glory of His activity. Everything rises to the heights of holiness.

In this, we acquire a guarantee that we will not be lowered and descend constantly downward, that we will not be transformed into a tool of death, destroying ourselves and others. The name of God must exist, and the light of His Torah that is given to earth, so as to accompany humanity through all its phases, so that we will not fall into that deep pit that already caused us to stumble in ancient days.

"And also you, in the blood of your covenant, I sent your prisoners forth from a pit that contained no water" (Zechariah 9:11).

Orot Hakodesh II, pp. 493-94

THE FOURFOLD SONG

There is a person who sings the song of his soul. He finds everything, his complete spiritual satisfaction, within his soul.

There is a person who sings the song of the nation. He steps forward from his private soul, which he finds narrow and uncivilized. He yearns for the heights. He clings with a sensitive love to the entirety of the Jewish nation and sings its song. He shares in its pains, is joyful in its hopes, speaks with exalted and pure thoughts regarding its past and its future, investigates its inner spiritual nature with love and a wise heart.

There is a person whose soul is so broad that it expands beyond the border of Israel. It sings the song of humanity. This soul constantly grows broader with the exalted totality of humanity and its glorious image. He yearns for humanity's general enlightenment. He looks forward to its supernal perfection. From this source of life, he draws all of his thoughts and insights, his ideals and visions.

And there is a person who rises even higher until he unites with all existence, with all creatures, and with all worlds. And with all of them, he sings. This is the person who, engaged in the Chapter of Song every day, is assured that he is a child of the World-to-Come.

And there is a person who rises with all these songs together in one ensemble so that they all give forth their voices, they all sing their songs sweetly, each supplies its fellow with fullness and life: the voice of happiness and joy, the voice of rejoicing and tunefulness, the voice of merriment and the voice of holiness.

The song of the soul, the song of the nation, the song of humanity, the song of the world—they all mix together with this person at every moment and at all times.

And this simplicity in its fullness rises to become a song of holiness, the song of God, the song that is simple, doubled, tripled, quadrupled, the song of songs of Solomon—of the king who is characterized by completeness and peace.

Orot Hakodesh II, p. 444

ALL OF THE PLAGUE HAS TURNED PURE WHITE

Within the totality of the world—
Both this-worldly and spiritual—
The only evil to be found
Is that which exists
In its isolated state.
But in the gathering of everything,
Everything is good—literally—
Not because evil is nullified into the majority
(As the desiccated accounting would have it),
But when seen from the perspective
Of the value
That is independent and ideal.

From this, you can understand
That to the degree
That the quantity of movement
Toward wholeness grows,
Evil decreases
And goodness is revealed.
Not only that,
But the gathering of evil in all its parts
Appears as the depths
Of a very great goodness,
Connecting in the depth of the heat of its yearning
To total goodness,

With which evil will not abide—
"All of the plague has turned pure white."

The life that is hidden
In this eternal point of view
Is what maintains the world,
Placing a bandage on the face
Of all destructive forces,
Not allowing them to cause
The world to totter.
"And he will guard heights upon heights."
Orot Hakodesh II, p. 454

OUR SOUL YEARNS FOR TOTAL GOODNESS

I.

What causes the continued presence of the idea of the existence of evil in the world?

Our point of view should be able to rise to a reckoning of a clear and inclusive world. It should be able to observe a totality that is good and complete.

The idea of the existence of evil is merely a diminution of the illumination that is filtered through various levels. As a result of that diminution, the soul asks: "Why can't everything be exalted, completely good and great?"

We might respond that a division into levels is necessary for the improvement of the world. But by saying so, we appeal to the idea of impossibility. We are claiming that it is impossible to bring about perfection without division into levels.

However, claiming that anything else than such a division is impossible impairs our appreciation of the supernal, our sense of the ultimate and infinite ability of the Creator of everything.

II.

When we arrive at the depth of the matter, we uproot the entirety of this misleading idea, this definitive statement regarding division into levels, which results in complaints about

the narrowness of reality.

There are two reasons for [complaint].

III.

The first reason [for complaint] is an internal one.

Through the true revelation of the all, the viewpoint of unity is revealed. In unity, everything is truly great and exalted, without any smallness or diminution whatsoever.

When our eye is weary, we see smallness and diminution. But even this has a [positive] consequence. We are impelled to examine the basis of goodness, greatness and light. We realize that our sense that greatness and light are the ultimate goodness and fulfillment is true—in its place. What is that place? Wherever it is fit that infinite greatness and goodness be revealed.

But there are also places where diminution is fitting.

There, diminution and smallness themselves comprise the complete and total goodness—just as greatness does in its place.

Then everything rises and returns to a state of total goodness, which doesn't require any measure of withholding.

The measure of withholding is a reality that appears dualistic: there are two aspects completing one other. One aspect is like the soul and the other like the body. Darkness perfects goodness, which is light. There is no day without night.

Day and night provide the basis for the perfection of the framework of time.

If not for the darkness, which presents the viewpoint of separation, there would be no drive toward continuous ascent.

That drive is basic. It perfects everything, until the quality of perfection in existence is no longer lacking: neither the [static] perfect quality that has no excess (and certainly no lack); nor the perfect quality that constantly adds perfection and that diffuses a constant, never-ending pleasure.

If not for the viewpoint of separation, we would only be aware of the quality of completeness. There would be no progress, no renewal of ascent.

And so the diminution, which causes the renewal of ascent, is literally complete good, like complete goodness itself. From the aspect of that diminution's ultimate supernal, infinite perfection, it has no connection to addition and ascent.

IV.

There remains only the feeling of pain and sorrow. We ask regarding this feeling: Why does it exist?

Sorrow is ameliorated in two ways.

The first is by accepting suffering with love. That is the level of supernal consciousness.

The second is by attaining a supernal viewpoint that transcends consciousness of belief in the quality of goodness.

V.

And so, everything is truly the measure of goodness, with no necessary conditions, no necessary circumstances.

This will certainly be revealed in the messianic future. At that time, we will make the blessing on everything, whether apparently good or bad, "He is good and does good." At that time, God's name [of compassion] will be pronounced just as it is written [when it indicates strictness].

VI.

Nevertheless, [there are] viewpoints that give credence to this withholding, with a proper appreciation for the supernal honor. These viewpoints have their place, once darkness exists. To the degree that these viewpoints reconcile our consciousness, their essence comes from the supernal light of truth that shines on those viewpoints.

All the bitterness and pain that we feel in those viewpoints comes from the foundation of darkness.

That darkness, however, is continuously transformed into great light.

Orot Hakodesh II, pp. 461-63

THERE IS NOTHING OLD

In the fullness of our soul, we sense the necessity of absolute goodness, the impossibility of its not existing, and the unceasing longing in the depths of our heart to rise to it, to approach its heights, to gaze upon its pleasantness.

We feel that the fulfillment of this absolute goodness in the completeness of its being—free of every boundary, of every condition and ordinance, of every definition and alteration—is a universal fulfillment.

The only way to fulfill our hopes for such goodness is to gaze—to the extent possible—upon the sparks of its radiance. Then strength and life, eternity and splendor shall descend to us and fill us.

After all this vision, we still remain thirsty for goodness to ascend. We still do not embrace the full circumference of goodness in its wholeness. We shall do so only when we shall see, besides the fulfillment of goodness, an ascent of goodness: a constant blossoming, an increase of strength, an ascent without limitations, without standstill.

The fulfillment of our ideal-oriented thirst will show us how to distinguish between the divine light and the worldly light, which draws life from its source.

The divine light satiates our exalted thirst for absolute goodness in its heights.

The worldly light, which grows ever brighter and which constantly rises, drawing from the life of its source, will satisfy us with the goodness of ascent, of increase of might, of additional rising—for which we so deeply thirst and yearn.

We will not be compelled to slake our thirst for knowledge and goodness—when they are united, making understood all existence, making knowable the secret of its ethical grandeur—with a dry conclusion that existence and decay are the final endpoint; a conclusion that leaves us mortified and shaken, filled with desperation about an on-going, unfolding process that depresses our spirit with the groan that "there is nothing new under the sun."

We rise above everything to the simple vision that our senses could grasp from existence only superficially. We step forward spiritually, striding higher than the sun. Then we pronounce that there is nothing old: everything blossoms, everything rises, everything constantly increases light and life.

Nor does the magnificent spirit fall when it sees that the path of ascent is circuitous, incorporating ascents and descents, advances and very great retreats—for the descents and retreats are filled with the spirit of ascent and advance.

The comprehension of this progress—as it approaches completion, becoming well-integrated in a knowledgeable, ethical life, as it is blessed and emerges from unripeness so that it is not eaten green—lifts the human spirit to the heights of divine light. It makes us assimilate within ourselves the inner goal of the knowledge of God—free of every ordinance and boundary—that exists within the treasure-house of the soul of Israel, that is revealed through the divine manifestation unique to Israel as the highest blossoming of the stream of light of the human soul in the midst of all the nations.

This constant progress fills us with an idealistic, ethical outlook on all of existence. It brings us to the fullness of a divine, knowing and comprehending light that unites our existence with the light of the Life of worlds, with the ultimate purity and ethics, strength and power in all their fullness.

The honor of God, wrapped in the breadth of creation in all its rich and varied hues, becomes known to us in its ideal radiance, growing constantly.

"May His great name be magnified and sanctified."

Orot Hakodesh II, pp. 466-67

AN ELIXIR OF LIFE AND A DRUG OF DEATH

The concept of evolution of existence and of all beings both depresses and elevates our spirit. Within ourselves, an elixir of life and a drug of death are immersed together.

When we turn to the past, we see the degradation that had existed then. We also see that as we stand now—morally, intellectually, physiologically—we surpass that past. Then in one regard, our mind grows self-satisfied; our moral restraints grow feeble. Regarding our present moral level, we claim—when struck by the evil spirit of some desire—that it is beyond our measure: much more than can be expected of creatures like us, who come from an animalistic nature and a coarse wildness.

In contrast, the outlook of evolution relating to the future exalts and elevates us: literally, to such a moral height that it is right that we think of ourselves in accordance with our understanding of the greatness of humanity at the beginning of its existence, of humanity's divine dwelling-place before its exile—in that primeval era—from the garden of Eden.

The more that we rise in knowledge and wisdom, in learning Torah and in good character traits, the more does our moral sense—intellectual and imaginative—soar. We proceed to the future. Automatically and continuously, the concept of evolution acts upon us, straightening our ways and supporting our moral faculties, until we enter palaces of holiness and purity with supernal might, filled with the power of God.

Then, the outlook of the past girds us with a strength of fear: we consider in our heart the terrible degradation of the past. We feel that if we disgrace our ways, we may fall back to that same dark degradation, rather than—by rectifying our ways and actions, private and communal—beholding a great light that shines forever, rising without end, substantial before us.

Orot Hakodesh II, p. 543

THE POWER THAT TURNS THE UNIVERSE

In the world, there exist gradual development and sudden leaps. There are soulful people whose character of leaping forward is stronger than their gradual growth.

This is the character of Jews: deeply influenced by the concept of teshuvah, yearning for the most exalted realities. Their surroundings and conditions may not be in concert with that. Nevertheless, their powerful yearning is the power that turns the universe, and gives forth the best wealth that may be found within life.

Orot Hakodesh II, p. 567

FROM *OROT HAKODESH*, VOLUME 3

THE ACTIONS OF EXALTED SOULS

Every action of exalted souls is united with their thoughts. This unity is great within them. Their actions are not symbolic, merely revealing their thoughts. Rather, their actions are literally revelations of life as those revelations appear on the level of the physical world. Those actions correspond literally to the revelation of thought within the world of intellect and thought.

All of this holy, exalted glory and beauty makes its appearance. It is a product of the supernal and wondrous unification in the heights o that exalted state. There, the lights and containers are of one material, one type, one being. He, His life-force and His self are one within them.

Then the words of such an exalted soul are alive, enduring, faithful and lovely—forever and ever.

Orot Hakodesh III, p. 96

THE INNER, ESSENTIAL "I"

"I am in the midst of the exile" (Ezekiel 1:1).

The inner, essential "I"—whether individual or communal—does not appear in and of itself. Rather, it appears in relation to our holiness and purity. It appears in relation to the amount of supernal power that, with the pure light of an elevated illumination, burns within us.

"Both we and our forefathers sinned" (Psalms 106:6).

This refers to the sin of Adam, who became alienated from his essence. He turned to the consciousness of the snake, and thus he lost himself. He could not clearly answer the question, "Where are you?", because he did not know himself, because he had lost his true "I."

He had bowed to a strange god.

And that was the sin of Israel, who "ran after foreign gods" (Deuteronomy 31:16). We abandoned our essential "I:" "Israel rejected goodness" (Hosea 8:3).

In the days of creation, the earth itself sinned. It denied its own essence.

It constricted its power, and went after limited goals and purposes. It did not give all of its hidden power so that the taste of the tree could be equal to the taste of its fruit.

Instead, it raised its eyes to look outside of itself. It considered a trivial future and way of being.

At that time as well, the moon complained. As a result, it lost its internal orbit, the joy of its portion. It was dreaming of a superficial beauty of royalty.

Thus does the world continue, sinking into the destruction of every "I"—of the individual and of the whole.

Learned educators come and focus on the superficial. They too remove their consciousness from the "I."

They add straw to the fire, give vinegar to the thirsty, and fatten minds and hearts with everything that is external to them.

And the "I" gets progressively forgotten.

And when there is no "I," there is no "He," and how much more is there no "You."

The Messiah is called "the breath of our nostrils, the anointed one of God" (Lamentations 4:20).

This is his might, the beauty of his greatness: that he is not outside of us. He is the breath of our nostrils.

Let us seek Hashem our God and David our king.

Let us tremble before God and His goodness.

Let us seek our "I."

Let us seek ourselves—and find.

Remove all foreign gods, remove every stranger and illegitimate one.

Then "you will know that I am Hashem your God, Who takes you out of the land of Egypt to be your God. I am Hashem."

Orot Hakodesh III, pp. 140-41

EVEN WHEN YOUR BODY IS BROKEN AND SHATTERED

Even when your body is broken and shattered and your spirit is dismayed and maimed because of so many miseries—spiritual and physical—spiritual pleasantness does not cease giving its honey and sweet influence. These soothe your spirit and give it an inner pleasure even in the midst of its darknesses. This sweetness is drawn by every one of us from our own outpouring of Torah and mitzvos: from performing them and from our intent when we do so.

Just as this applies to each one of us, so does it apply to the entire Jewish nation, which draws constantly from the sweet goodness of the inner holiness of the pleasantness of God, which sweetens life and pours forth a pattern that has achieved honor and rectification.

Then life is filled with a content of inner satisfaction in the depth of the universal soul of the community of Israel, whose rays and sparks of light stream toward every one of us, according to how much we have cultivated on our soul's illumination, and according to the extent of our inner connection to the whole.

Orot Hakodesh III, p. 174

TO LOVE THIS WORLD WELL

To love this world well, we must submerge ourselves deeply in the love of the world-to-come. We must carry out all the improvements of this world in the most comprehensive way possible. These in fact are comprehensive preparations for the sake of each detail and the complete entirety of the life of the world-to-come.

Only then will culture stride forward with confidence.

This is a great wisdom, which is known to faith. This wisdom is so great that it will ultimately conquer the entire world.

When despair fills each soul and the life of this world is devalued, then the love of the world-to-come approaches, offering the dew of life that will vivify the life of this world.

Elders and youth will gaze towards it together, and shine.

And kings and ministers, fighters and warriors, will find within it the source of the rich dew of their lives.

Orot Hakodesh III, p. 178

THE HOLY MIXTURE OF PLEASURE AND JOY

When humility and awe are revealed, they bring forth pleasantness and joy. Refined pleasure comes from the foundation of humility, and pure joy from the foundation of awe. And the revelation of the countenances of these illuminated visions results from the influence of their lights upon each other: "I call to them to stand together." From the holy mixture of these branches comes a supernal might, extremely powerful, which motivates all aspects of life with a holy grandeur.

Orot Hakodesh III, p. 187

THE SOURCE OF DELIGHT

In the land of Israel, it is possible to draw the joy of holiness from the site of joy itself. Outside the land, however, it is impossible to draw down this joy, because of the opposition and wrath of the powers of judgement outside the land. We can draw down this joy only by drawing it from the source of delight, where neither obstacle nor damage reach. This is why, in consequence of the destruction of the temple, "joy" is halachically forbidden, but those things called "delight" are allowed.

When we delight in love from the delights of the source of holiness, there descends a pure joy, enriched with delight, which draws the atmosphere of the land of Israel—to some degree—outside the land, to revive the spirit of those who hope for the mercies of God, who yearn to see it and to rejoice in its joy.

"Recall me, Hashem, when you desire your nation, visit me with Your salvation...to rejoice in the joy of your nation, to take pride in Your inheritance" (Tehillim 106:4-5).

Orot Hakodesh III, p. 187

THE POETIC SOUL

If your soul is poetic,
You must be acquainted with your character,
Your special longings, desires,
The path of your soul
And the special spiritual food it requires
To satisfy its spiritual life—
Just as air is required to breathe.
You may join with other gifted people
For other spiritual necessities.
But never forget that you are summoned
To stand firm
Upon your own spiritual foundation.
Regarding all service of God,
All discussion, teachings, examinations, analyses, logic—
From your spirit,
Which is pure and powerful,
Filled with a song that is holy, alive and unblemished,
Sprinkle upon them
Pure streams of light,
Expressions of song,
Elevation of the soul,
Which desires constantly
Her beloved, her redeemer:
The living God.

When the poetic, sensitive soul
Gazes upon supernal matters of greatness

Before they have been put in order for her
And well-arranged,
She descends to an activism
Regarding finite, this-worldly matters.
She is susceptible at every step to enthusiasms
Whose particular character is falsehood.
At such a time, an exalted individual
Must find the inspiring foundation
From which that spirit of falsehood comes forth
So poetically,
And rectify its character internally,
Without expressing the spirit in unavailing words.
Then the idea proceeds,
Reflecting heavenly matters of greatness.
In this context, the greatest exaggeration
Merely indicates the smallest expression
Of what heaven is.

And if then, from the midst of the flow of spirit
That constantly ascends,
Rising beyond all boundaries,
There are still, at times,
Obvious mis-statements,
These are "an error that appears to come
From the Ruler of the world" (Ecclesiastes 10:5).
They too have their purpose.
Such this-worldly words
Shall be a source of blessing
And learning.
Orot Hakodesh III, p. 215

A PERFECT PRAYER

People may abandon prayer because they envision a perfect prayer, a brightly radiant prayer. Even though this abandonment is a great loss, when that bright prayer does arrive, it restores the entire loss. This is so in regard to an individual or the community: the entire congregation of Israel.

Prayer will come to the people of Israel. It will come in a very bright form, a form that flows from the midst of the entirety of its soul, from the midst of its inner awareness, from the midst of its view of the world, and from the midst of all its influence upon the world in the past, present and future.

When that prayer of the people of Israel comes, the entire world will be astonished at its glory and splendor, its strength and grace. It will come from the midst of that perfect will that makes the entire world one bloc of holiness, that turns all of life into one chapter of supernal song, a new song, a song of Hashem upon the land of Israel, a song of Zion redeemed and filled with eternal redemption.

Involving ourselves in Perek Shirah—the song of all creation—is the foundation of the service of wisdom, a service filled with eternal life, flowing directly from an immediate union between the human and all existence. This is the precursor to the standard service of God, which comes to humanity by means of the Torah.

Orot Hakodesh III, p. 227

TORAH AND GOOD DEEDS

Torah and good deeds
Purify your character.
But you cannot rely on this alone.
You must work on your character.
In particular,
You must perfect your ethical being.
Orot Hakodesh III, p. 233

FROM THE DEPTHS OF CHAOS

The call to purify your character never ceases.

You may have already purified it when you were on an intermediate spiritual level.

But when you grow, you bring hidden treasures of life out of the depths of chaos. These portions come to you as a spiritual revelation. Because they have never been refined, they require constantly new purifying.

There are holy people who never cease growing. They go from strength to strength, always engaged in actualized repentance.

Purifying and refining character is a vital ingredient of that repentance.

Orot Hakodesh III, p. 233

CONSOLATION FOR EVERY MONSTROUS VISION

At times, your soul is revealed to you in all its naked ugliness—and you are repulsed by the vision. But only in this way can you calm your spirit: for corresponding to the ugliness of the soul and its impurity, so will its beauty and purity grow. "One corresponding to the other did God create them."

After you strengthen yourself and rise beyond the shocking vision of that aspect of ugliness—so that the aspect of purity shines before your eyes, the aspect of the beauty within your soul; and your eyes, seeing, are illumined—then you will gain consolation for every monstrous vision that had terrified you. "The humble will increase their joy in God, and the most impoverished will rejoice in the Holy One of Israel" (Isaiah 29:19).

Orot Hakodesh III, p. 251

PEARLS

When you sense that you have fallen because the spirit of your ethical awareness is weak,

consider this: you have to draw forth precious pearls from the depths of the abyss.

When you know this, then you will rise. You will renew your abilities with strength and tranquility. You will approach the ever-lasting light with more capability than you ever had before.

This rule applies to the entire generation. It governs reality forever.

Orot Hakodesh III, p. 252

REALMS OF DARKNESS

When you feel humiliated, empty, lacking all spiritual strength, when you fall and stumble, realize that a great light is prepared for you.

All of your imperfections and all the damage that you have caused–this-worldly, spiritual, things you did or didn't do throughout your life–they all stand before you. Everything you ever did wrong testifies against you.

You are stunned. You feel great anguish, and from the midst of that anguish you experience regret.

Then you will rise up and repent. You will rise up from the depth of the abyss to the elevated pinnacle, from impurity to purity, from blackness to a great light.

As you emerge and rise, you will have to pass through realms of darkness that overwhelm you and eclipse you.

But be aware that "God is merciful and gracious," that "even though I walk through the valley of the shadow of death, I shall not fear evil, for God is with me."

When you cry out to God from the midst of the confusions of the abyss, your voice will be heard.

When you call out for the light of knowledge, it will shine on you.

Wisdom and kindness will support you and crown you. You will swiftly return to the citadel, filled with wisdom, joy and strength. [the citadel is filled with these, or the person?]

Orot Hakodesh III, p. 252

THE SEXUAL DRIVE STREAMS INTO THE FUTURE

The sexual drive streams into the future, to the perfection of life that time will bring: the life of the world-to-come within this world. That future life is filled with complete beauty and pleasure; thus, great is the yearning and the strength of desire of the sexual drive, which is all-encompassing; only upon this drive does ultimate holiness rest its light.

The pure soul leads the sexual drive to its goal within the boundary of Torah, wisdom, rectitude and modesty: the sources of righteousness. "Whoever guards the covenant is called righteous."

The basis of the holiness of Israel is tied to the world of the future. A holy spirit continuously embraces the entirety of the nation and its individuals. "Your people are all righteous."

Orot Hakodesh III, p. 296

THE PERFECTION OF LIFE THAT TIME WILL BRING

Thought is the eternal revelation of each human being. It is disclosed in speech. Thought pours forth, flowing directly from the eternal aspect of sexuality into the procreative faculty colored by the context of one's life.

In accordance with how your elevated thought, in its purity, shines upon your power of speech, the essential strength of life in your sexuality will be elevated and enveloped in supernal holiness. The inner light of life in all its strength will shine through your power of speech: "You shall command and it will come about; light shall shine upon your path" (Job 22:28)

Orot Hakodesh III, p. 296

THE WORLD OF HUMANITY

A supernal ethical gaze flows from supernal consciousness of the divine. It places its seal on the nexus where God's will and the ultimate purpose of sexuality join. That seal is the eternal and infinite aspect of sexuality concealed in one's human character. In this invaluable point, all supernal pleasures are concealed.

There exists a precious strategy whose goal is to rectify this holy foundation, to turn sexuality and its essential offshoots to the holy goal of life. That strategy is the cornerstone of all ethical values. It establishes the world of humanity, both internal and external.

Days will come when the general culture will gaze with exalted appreciation at the divine glory pervading those thoughts that now appear benighted to those who are sexually gross, who have an unrefined consciousness, who remain outside the camp of Israel. Those thoughts are connected, in the mystic aspect of ethics, to sexual rectification, to all the fast-day prayers and outcries of those who have strayed. "Light is sown for the righteous, and to those who have an honest heart, joy."

Orot Hakodesh III, p. 296

THE PLAGUE WILL NOT ENTER YOUR TENT

You can profoundly rectify your mis-spent sexuality by sanctifying your will and illuminating it clearly, until the light of holiness will stream through even your strongest physical drive. That drive is rooted in holiness that is incredibly strong, because it contains the expression of life: the sexual drive. The light of holiness will stream within it to such a degree that its holy aspect will rule your life and direct its action and expression. Then sexuality's secular aspect, and certainly its unclean aspect, will be totally nullified before its holy aspect. Then, in truth, the plague will not enter your tent; you shall be righteous and guarded from stumbling.

Orot Hakodesh III, p. 298

WHEN YOUR WILL RISES

When your will rises to that supernal level of holiness, it is cleared of all bad traits and all bad actions that exist in the world—even of the most inconsequential matters that most people ignore.

One might desire illicit relations more than life itself, because sexual relations are embedded in one's drive to give life to all generations. But through sexual holiness, you can rise to the level and archetype of the righteous man of all generations.

Similarly, one might experience the desire to steal: for what one possesses can support generations to come as an inheritance. the love of evil acquisition exceedingly degrades one's care for future generations. But the goodness within holiness can rise to the heights of life and elevate it.

Orot Hakodesh III, p. 298

HOLINESS IN ACTION AND HOLINESS IN THOUGHT

Holiness in action and holiness in thought anchor the holiness of nature and will in its very foundation. The sexual act is sanctified in the strength of a pure and holy nature. This was the human experience before the sin. This all-encompassing holiness and, even higher than that, the longing for this holiness refine your entire connection to your soul. Familial relations are bound with the threads of the holy of holies, so strong and powerful, bringing a flow of long life to your descendants.

From this saintly basis flow life and refinement, power and strength, the greatness of life. All of your life is filled with strength: for those who are with you, for the generation, for the entire world.

Strength adds to strength, life draws forth life. Honor and beauty cause beauty and the glory of holiness to shine upon all.

Orot Hakodesh III, p. 299

THE PRECIOUS REASON FOR CIRCUMCISION

The precious reason for circumcision, which decreases sexual desire, encompasses broad principles of wisdom. The covenant—"to be a God to you and to your children after you"—offers knowledge of God's oneness, which is connected to circumcision. The covenant and circumcision are intimately intertwined.

"From his flesh does a man see God." If you have the power to harness all the abilities of your soul and all your drives to an enlightened and ethical goal, you will see unity in your internal world. The unity of the outer world will become increasingly clear to you. But if your abilities are splintered, if you cannot conceive of overall control of your drives and desires, you will conclude that the entire world, like you, is splintered, and that no unity can be found in existence.

Sexual desire in its essence—and in related expressions, physical, imaginative and spiritual—comprises the basis of all drives. If you experience sexuality in a way that your exalted spirit can rise to it and surround it, can unify it with all the wealth of human abilities (physical and spiritual), leading it to one integrated ethical and supernal goal, then that unity, in its power, is revealed. the revelation of Godly unity will appear in your flesh.

The total immersion of the human spirit in sexual desire to such a degree that the ideals and ethics in its realm are silenced has brought about the substance of the foreskin. This pathological state expresses itself physically as a powerful sexual drive that has left the realm of ideals and the transmission of the ultimate ethics.

Pessimism corresponds to ethical decline. It gives urgency to the divorce of sexual desire from idealism: since existence in general is such a great evil, how can the procreation of miserable creatures be ideal? This doctrine teaches that the sexual drive is not rooted in idealism, but merely demonstrates the eruption of desire.

How different is the outlook of general goodness, of optimism: "God saw all that He had made, and behold, it was very good." This view permits idealism to extend even over the sexual drive.

The nature of flesh and the inclination of one's heart can descend to the degraded state of the foreskin. But with circumcision, you rectify the holy covenant and stride on an exalted path. All your abilities are directed toward a goal that is all-inclusive, ideal and holy. From your flesh will you see God. You will sanctify the Holy One of Israel, the one God.

Orot Hakodesh III, p. 300

BE GOOD TO ALL

When you experience a strong desire to be good to all, realize that an illumination from the supernal world has come to you. How fortunate you will be if you prepare a proper place in your heart, in your mind, in the acts of your hands and in all your feelings to receive this exalted guest, which is greater and more exalted than the most noble of this earth. Take hold of it and do not let go.

Do not allow any delays and obstacles—whether physical or spiritual—that hinder you from taking this holy inspiration into yourself to stop you. Fight for everything. Rise in your strength. Lift your consciousness to the far reaches and imitate the qualities of God, Who is good to all and Whose compassion encompasses all His creatures.

Orot Hakodesh III, p. 316

THE LIBERATED LIGHT

From the well of kindness, your love for humanity must burst forth—not as an unreasoned commandment, for then it would lose the most clear aspect of its brilliance, but as a powerful movement of the spirit within you.

This love must withstand very difficult challenges. It must overcome many contradictions, which are scattered like boulders upon which you may stumble. These are found in isolated Torah statements, in the superficial aspect of some Torah laws, and in a multitude of points of view that stem from the constriction within the revealed aspect of the Torah and the national ethical sense.

It is clear that when the love of humanity grows remote from its divine source, its blossom withers.

And the divine source expresses its light through the conduits of Torah and mitzvah, and through the definition of the Jewish nation as unique.

All this requires the effort of a great spirit: how to maintain these conduits where they stand, and yet draw the waters of kindness in their original purity and breadth.

Again and again, we must descend to the depths of darkness in order to excavate—precisely from there—the most liberated light, the greatest and most elevated.

Orot Hakodesh III, p. 318

THE INCLUSIVE PATH OF GOD

A person who is connected with love to the totality of existence, desiring its rectification and goodness, is also connected to the wicked and wrongdoers within it.

This creates the possibility of damaging the holiness of his pure soul, which desires only holiness and true goodness.

Still, the spirit of the tzaddik, who loves all of existence, grows so strongly with love of all creatures, love of humanity, and, in particular, the love of Israel, that nothing repels him—not even the fear that he himself will become spiritually flawed.

At last, he refines himself so much that he connects himself to the essence of goodness of all existence—everything.

In truth, all existence is always good: "Hashem is good to all."

By means of this love, he rises even higher.

And by means of that spiritual elevation, all of existence rises, until even the evil particulars of the entirety become progressively perfected.

They do so by means of the connection of the spirit of the tzaddik—who truly loves everything—with them.

A person whose way of service this is must refine himself a great deal.

He must be quick and careful so that his actions, thoughts and all his feelings are really given over to the good of all existence. This is really what we can understand of the description of the will of God.

Then, his spiritual thought unites with the oneness of existence, and "evil shall not come upon it."

However, it may be that someone comes to connect himself to the love of all, but his spirit is dark within him with his own personal motives. Even though he also contains pure sparks of the love of all, his own soul is not properly centered and united.

This means that his connection with all existence is not solid.

It is possible that his connection is directed to the degraded and evil aspect of all existence. The goodness and chosen in the totality of existence will grow far from connecting with his soul.

Then, this connection is truly flawed.

That is why we find a natural sense in many people, people who fear God and learn Torah, of only wanting to connect with the love of good people and with the chosen nation.

In truth, this is a fine path for all those who have not properly refined themselves.

But this is not the path of God that is fit for those whose souls are perfected, for those who have the power to refine themselves and their motives.

Such people are obligated, in addition to the special love for the chosen people, to love all existence and to hope for its complete salvation, for the salvation of all particulars of the all with no division whatsoever.

If such people find in themselves any descent or spiritual eclipse resulting from their connection to the totality of existence because of its degraded parts, they do not turn back from the inclusive path of God that is fit for them.

Instead, they hurry to acquire the proper refinement, so that they will be able to be connected to all of existence, from the aspect of the essence of the goodness of Hashem—the true goodness, which rests in Him.

Then their exalted love will not damage them or cause them to descend.

It will allow them to ascend, and it will give them additional purity, strength and holiness.

Orot Hakodesh III, pp. 319-20

THE SUPERNAL TREASURE

Some people are so saintly, so great is their tendency toward supernal holiness, that their hearts are empty of any love for this world. They lack even that portion of love for this world that is fit to exist in a person's heart.

As a result, they find imperfection in their human character, and they cannot be leaders in this world.

And so they must retrieve their love for this world. They do so through prayer, which deals with impermanent things; and through the in-depth study of Jewish law and this-worldly discussions of the Torah, in all their detailed ramifications. Then they have a love for the world that becomes a love of holiness, and which unites with the love of Torah.

Through these people, the world is elevated.

As far as these supernal tzaddikim, these individuals of the spirit, are concerned, the things of this world can claim no place of importance. These people correctly assess what the supernal treasure and illumination is, and their intent is to cultivate it continuously and draw it into the entire world.

It is an absolute truth that their service is not at all the same as the paths of service of others, who are constantly enclosed within the confines of this world and its desires, within the prisons of the body and its proclivities. When we see something in them that astonishes us, we should have no critical thoughts, for all their ways flow from a very exalted holiness.

Orot Hakodesh III, p.305

THE PURPOSE OF EVIL

We see the evil within the individual and in the life of human society. We find that with all its negativity and evil, it has a purpose—a temporary purpose. Evil contains particular power, the might of will and the depths of life. These are necessary components with which to perfect virtue and goodness. And we are assured that in the end, the evil will pass. The individual will be perfected and society will be perfected. Then everything will stand upon the basis of goodness. Evil will evaporate, and the yearning of evil, the wrath, the murder, the coarseness, and all their offshoots, will evaporate like smoke.

The same process applies to the entire world.

Without any doubt, this power of evil hungering for evil causes upheaval in the world. It rules and is filled with force, all the days of evil, as long as the world requires the evil upheaval, the universal evil-doer hungers, with all his branches, to exterminate and destroy, to poison and pollute, to darken and blacken, to separate and explode. And he extends his evil until the final time, until the world will be perfected, until a new spirit, a spirit of pure life, will breathe upon human beings, when holy souls will awaken for the endeavor of true liberation, and take refuge the kingdom of supernal holy ones.

Everything mentioned in the words of the sages—all their puzzling sayings regarding evil and its existence, regarding its temporary power and force, regarding its destruction and annihilation in the end of days—it is all is sealed in a writing of truth.

Orot Hakodesh III, p. 478

FROM *OROT HAKODESH*, VOLUME 4

THE LIGHT OF LIFE

Exacting care in our actions inspired by the lower wellspring—the fear of punishment—may contain small-mindedness and judgements.

Ultimately, this will rise. Ultimately, all its strictness will become a flame of holy might: with love and a fire that blazes with the pleasantness of divine friendship; with love of humanity; with grace and good wisdom.

Ultimately, this exacting attitude will arrive at the supernal wellspring of the light of life. There, the illumination of holy pleasures shines the might of its radiance upon life.

"God, how precious Your kindness is!
In the shadow of Your wing,
People find sanctuary.
They are gratified by the wealth of Your home.
You give them to drink from Your river of delight.

The wellspring of life is with You.
And so, in Your light, we will see light.

Extend Your kindness to those who know You,
And Your justice to those who are honest" (Psalms 36:8-10).
Orot Hakodesh IV, p. 419

THE FEAR OF GOD

In every clash, whether physical or spiritual, we experience light and its vessel: the soul and body. In accordance with the clarity of our understanding and the purity of our will, so does light shine upon us from the vessel. Our soul shines from our body.

When our thoughts tumble over one another, there is one universal treasury: the fear of God, the fear of punishment and an ordinary trepidation.

This constitutes the floor of that tabernacle of faith that stretches out to rectify the world.

Then, in accordance with the clarity of our understanding and the holiness of our acts and our spirit, our soul is revealed.

Our soul had been steeped in the midst of that corporeal and crude fear.

Now our soul is revealed: our soul, which is the crown of all spiritual ideals, of the glory of honor and of the awe of God's greatness. It is the stronghold of love. It is the source of the streams of all idealistic yearnings, mighty in their desire, which rise higher and higher to the most elevated worlds.

Orot Hakodesh IV, p. 420

EMPTINESS

There are souls to whom clinging to the divine is the foundation of their life. When they maintain only a minimal involvement with the Torah and its commandments, they feel a depth of suffering that stems from an emptiness affecting the quality of their souls.

Such people are able to comprehend the great destruction wrought by evil-doers, those who forget God.

Such people can comprehend to what a degree these evil people's image is marred, and how truly pitiable they are—these people who, wise in their own eyes and believing that they lack nothing, follow the dictates of their evil heart.

Orot Hakodesh IV, p. 447

CLOSING WORDS

The Glory of All

I love all;
I cannot but love all:
All the nations.
From my very depth, I want the glory of all,
The perfection of all.
My love to Israel burns more greatly
And is deeper,
But this inner desire spreads out in the force of its love
To all.
I have no need at all to force this feeling of love--
It wells directly from the holy depth of Wisdom
Of the Godly soul.
Arpelei Tohar 22

Made in the USA
Coppell, TX
12 May 2022